BEGINNING HISTORY

EGYPTIAN PYRAMIDS

Anne Steel

Illustrated by John James

The Bookwright Press
New York · 1990

BEGINNING HISTORY

Crusaders
Egyptian Pyramids
Greek Cities
Norman Castles

*J
932
Ste*

All words that appear in **bold** are explained in the glossary on page 22

First published in the United States in 1990 by
The Bookwright Press, 387 Park Avenue South, New York, NY 10016

First published in 1989 by Wayland (Publishers) Limited, 61 Western Road, Hove, East Sussex, BN3 1JD

© Copyright 1989 Wayland (Publishers) Ltd

Library of Congress Cataloging-in- Publication Data
Steel, Anne.
Egyptian pyramids/by Anne Steel.
p. cm. – (Beginning history)
Bibliography: p.
Includes index.
Summary: Discusses the famous pyramids of Egypt, how they were built, and how they were
involved in the religious beliefs and burial practices of the ancient Egyptians.
ISBN 0–531–18325–4
1. Pyramids – Egypt – Juvenile literature. 2. Funeral rites and ceremonies. Ancient – Egypt –
Juvenile literature. [1. Pyramids – Egypt. 2. Egypt – Antiquities]
I. Title.   II. Series: Beginning history (New York, N.Y.)
DT63.S68 1990   89–35176
932 – dc20   CIP
                                                        AC

Typeset by Kalligraphics Limited, Horley, Surrey
Printed in Italy by G. Canale & C.S.p.A., Turin

CONTENTS

ANCIENT EGYPT

About seven thousand years ago, the Egyptians began to build villages along the banks of the Nile River. These villages soon grouped together into **tribes**, and each tribe had its own leader. By 3200 BC all the tribes were ruled by one king called the pharaoh. This was the beginning of the Kingdom of Egypt.

The most important influence in the Egyptians' lives was the Nile River. It gave them water to **irrigate** their crops, and fish and water birds to eat. When they wanted to travel or move goods, they sailed their boats on the river.

The Ancient Egyptians believed in a life after death and prepared very carefully for it. When a pharaoh was buried, many treasures were buried with him to take to the next world. Huge stone pyramids were built to honor the dead pharaoh and to protect the **tomb** and its treasures from thieves.

A busy scene on the Nile River with pyramids in the background.

THE NEXT WORLD

Egyptians believed that life after death would be spent in a kingdom ruled by Osiris, god of the dead. Life there was like life in this world, so people were buried with objects that would be useful to them in the next world. Statues were placed in the tomb, and pictures of everyday life were painted on the walls. At the

A pharaoh's tomb was filled with statues, paintings and treasures to take with him to the next world.

The tomb and coffin of a pharaoh.

burial, special prayers were said that were believed to make the body come to life.

Egyptians believed that the dead traveled to the next world by boat across the River of Death. A Book of the Dead was left in the tomb with maps and magic passwords to help them find their way. The dead person entered the Hall of Judgement, where the heart was weighed against the feather of truth. If the heart weighed the same as the feather, the person could pass into the next world; but if it was heavier, the person was judged to be evil and fed to a terrible monster.

Some of the furniture found in the tomb of a pyramid at Giza.

7

FAMOUS PYRAMIDS

Above The inside of a mastaba showing statues and wall paintings.

The earliest Egyptian graves were very simple and could easily be broken into and robbed. To prevent this, the Egyptians began to build tombs called mastabas. These were rectangular buildings placed over a **burial chamber**. Pharaohs had mastabas built with many rooms inside to protect the burial chamber from thieves, but the graves were still robbed.

The first pyramid was built for Pharaoh Zoser at Sakkara. There were six huge steps built on top of the tomb

Right The step pyramid at Sakkara.

to make it safer from robbers. The Pharaoh's spirit was believed to have climbed the steps of the pyramid to the stars. Later pyramids were built without steps, like the famous group at Giza. The largest of these is the Great Pyramid, built for Pharaoh Khufu. Each side is 450 feet (144 m) high and measures 756 feet (230 m) at the base. It would have taken at least twenty years to build.

Thieves robbing a royal tomb.

THE PYRAMID BUILDERS

Many thousands of people were needed to build a pyramid. Some of them, such as the **architect** and planners, were highly skilled. Their plans had to be accepted by the pharaoh before any work could begin. **Quarry** men were needed to get the stone out of the ground, and **masons** worked to shape the rough stone. Painters decorated the walls inside the tomb, and **sculptors** made statues and carvings.

The heavy work of moving the stones was done by people with no special building skills. Some of them were farmers who had to leave their land for some time each year when the Nile flooded. Others may have been prisoners, or people paying **labor tax** to the pharaoh. As there was no money in Ancient Egypt, the workers were paid with food, wine, clothes and other goods.

A busy scene at the site of a new pyramid. A supervisor is watching to make sure the work is done properly.

The burial chamber and stone coffin inside the Great Pyramid at Giza.

THE BUILDING BLOCKS

The Great Pyramid was built with over two million blocks of stone. Many of the stones came from a quarry in the desert nearby. Each one weighed up to two tons, and it was a huge task to cut them and move them to where the pyramid was being built. The stones were cut out of the ground with wooden, copper or stone tools. Grooves were made in the stone and wooden wedges driven into them. Water was then poured over the wedges, which swelled up and split the stone into pieces.

The famous pyramids at Giza.

Some of the stones were taken to the site of the pyramid by boat, while others were carried on **sledges**, which were dragged across the sand by gangs of men. Once the stones arrived at the pyramid, masons shaped each one carefully so that it fitted perfectly into place. This was very important, especially for the stones that made up the smooth sloping sides.

The great stone blocks were carried by boat from the quarries to the pyramid site.

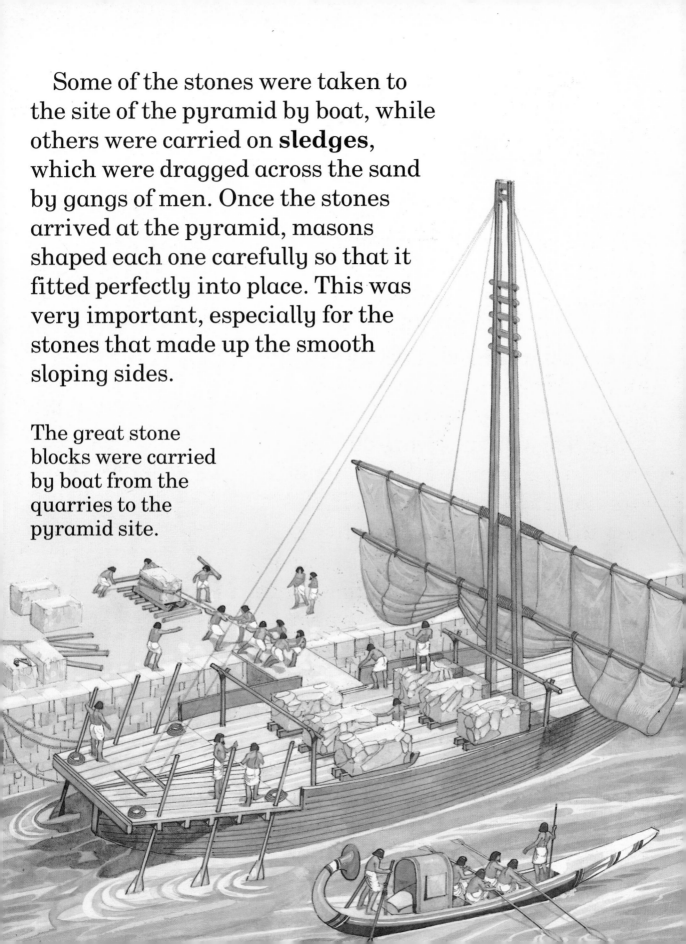

Beginning The Work

Once the pharaoh had agreed to the plans of his pyramid, the **foundations** could be laid. There was often a special foundation ceremony, which the pharaoh sometimes attended. The plan of the building was marked out on the ground with wooden stakes and string. Then ditches were dug and water was poured into them to make sure that they were level. Stones were then laid down in the ditches.

After the first layer of stones was laid, a mud ramp was built up so that the workmen could reach the next level. A new ramp was added for each layer of stones. The smoother white **facing** stones were placed on the outsides of the pyramid as the work was finished and the ramps removed. The painters and sculptors then set to work inside the pyramid to prepare the tomb and burial chamber.

HIDING THE TOMB

Inside, the pyramid was a maze of passages and rooms. The main aim of the builders was to hide the burial chamber so that thieves could not steal its treasures. The entrance was usually on the north side of the pyramid and it was always well hidden. Inside, the passages might lead to false burial chambers or dead

The main passages inside a pyramid, showing false passageways and dead ends.

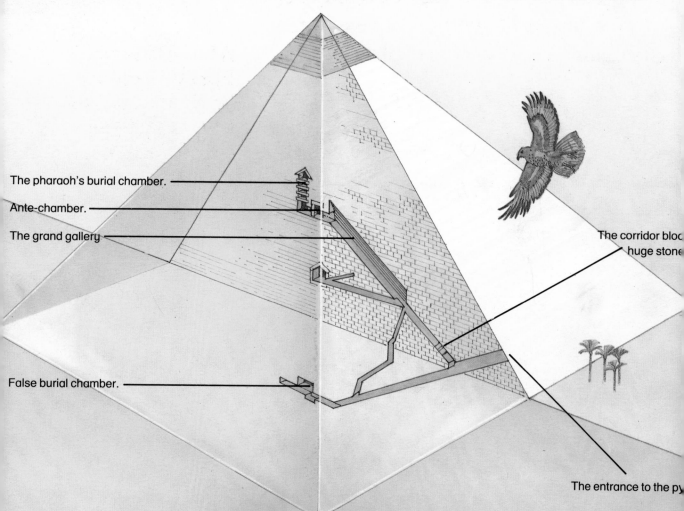

The pharaoh's burial chamber.

Ante-chamber.

The grand gallery

The corridor bloc huge stone

False burial chamber.

The entrance to the py

ends. In the Great Pyramid there was a false chamber underground. The real chamber was blocked off with huge stone slabs. But this was not enough to keep robbers from stealing everything except the stone tomb.

Inside the burial chambers the painters drew a **grid** on the wall and then copied pictures from a plan drawn on a piece of **papyrus**. The work had to be done very carefully because the Egyptians believed that the scenes would come to life when the dead pharaoh was sealed inside.

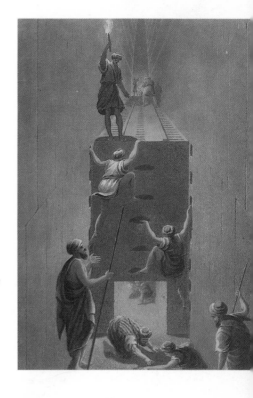

Above The way from the second level to the third level inside the Great Pyramid.

Left Scenes of everyday life painted on the walls of a pharaoh's tomb.

PREPARING THE BODY

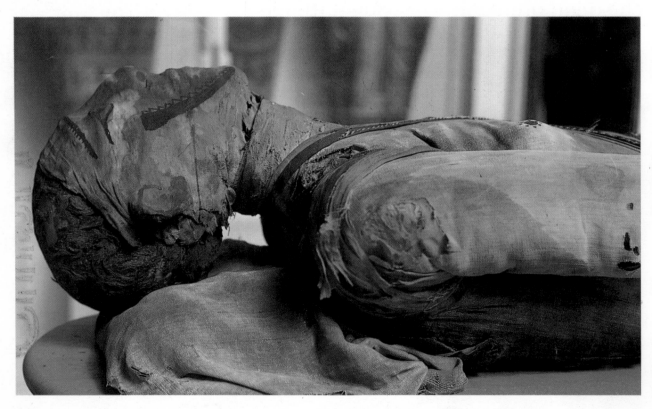

Ancient Egyptian mummies.

The Egyptians had a special way of wrapping bodies in linen bandages which made them last for thousands of years. We call these bodies "mummies." When an important person died, the body was taken to the **embalmers** for about seventy days. The insides were taken out and placed in special jars called canopic jars. The body was covered with

natron and left to dry. After about forty days it was washed and the inside of the body was packed with linen. The body was wrapped in many layers of linen bandages that were coated with oil and **resin**. The head was fitted with a decorated mask and the mummy was placed in a wooden or plaster coffin. The coffin was then painted with beautiful pictures of gods and goddesses. Sometimes three coffins were placed one inside another.

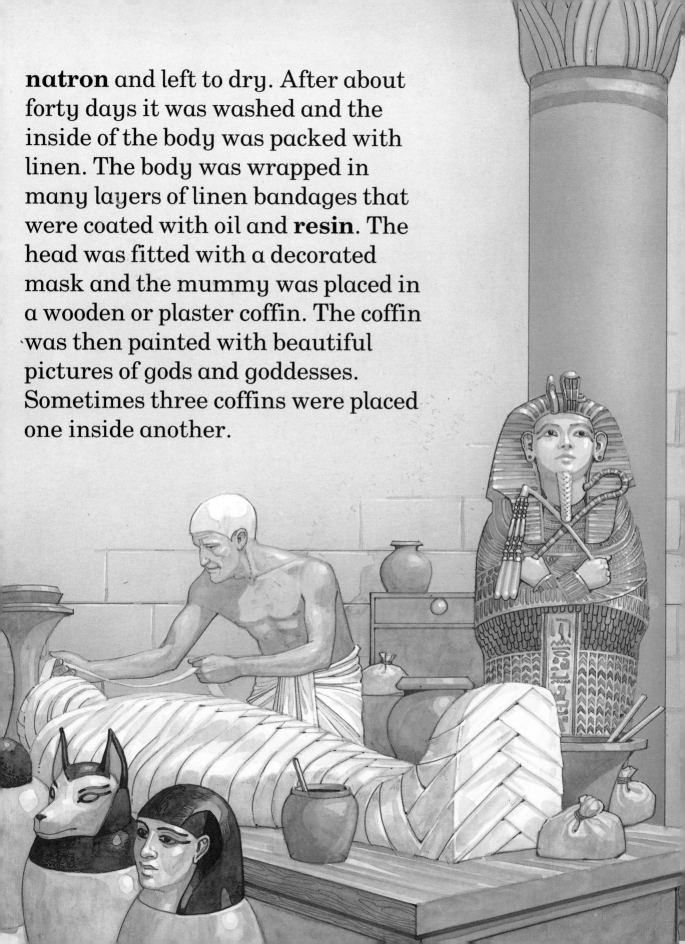

A ROYAL BURIAL

Every pharaoh was given a very grand burial. When his body had been prepared, the mummy was put in the coffin and carried by a sledge shaped like a boat, which was pulled by oxen. The canopic jars were carried on another sledge.

The priests and priestesses led the **mourners**. They were followed by servants carrying all the things the pharaoh would need for his new life, such as furniture, food and clothes. They also carried statues of servants which would come to life and work for the pharaoh in the next world. At the entrance to the pyramid a priest

A royal burial, showing the pharaoh's coffin being taken by sledge to its last resting place.

opened the mummy's mouth with a special tool. The Egyptians believed that this gave the dead person the power to speak, eat and breathe again. The coffin was put in the tomb and sealed in an underground burial chamber deep inside the pyramid.

Today, all of the thirty or so pyramids of Ancient Egypt have lost their treasures. But the pyramids themselves still stand, reminding us of Egypt's rich and colorful history.

GLOSSARY

Architect A person who designs and makes plans for buildings.

Burial chamber A closed-in room where the pharaohs were placed in their tombs.

Embalmers People who prepared dead bodies for burial so as to keep them from decaying.

Facing An outer layer of material put on a surface for protection.

Foundations The base and support of a building, usually below ground.

Grid A set of lines crisscrossed to form a pattern of equal squares.

Irrigate To supply water to land to help produce good crops.

Labor tax A tax paid to the pharaoh in the form of work instead of goods.

Masons People skilled in working with stone.

Mourners People who feel sadness at the death of somebody.

Natron A salt-like powder used to dry and preserve a body.

Papyrus A kind of paper made from reeds.

Quarry An area that is dug to take stone, clay, marble, etc. from the ground.

Resin A substance that comes from plants.

Sculptors People who make carvings and statues out of wood, marble, stone, etc.

Sledge A sled used for transporting heavy loads.

Tomb A room or heavy stone box, usually underground, for the dead.

Tribes Large groups of people and their animals.

BOOKS TO READ

Ancient Egypt by Susan Purdy and Cass R. Sandak (A Civilization Project Book). Franklin Watts, 1982

Ancient Egypt by Rosalie and Anthony David. Warwick, 1984

Ancient Egypt, Rev. Edn. by Miriam Stead. Gloucester, 1985

Ancient Egypt, Rev. Edn. by Charles Alexander Robinson, Jr. Franklin Watts, 1984.

Cleopatra and the Egyptians by Andrew Langley. Bookwright, 1986

Egypt by Ann Millard. Franklin Watts, 1988

Science in Ancient Egypt by Geraldine Woods. Franklin Watts, 1988

See Inside an Egyptian Town, Rev. Edn. by R. J. Unstead. Warwick, 1986

Picture Acknowledgments

The publishers would like to thank the following for providing the photographs in this book: Mary Evans Picture Library 12 (top and bottom); Ronald Sheridan's Ancient Art & Architecture 6, 18 (top); Werner Forman Archive Ltd 7 (bottom), 8 (top and bottom); Zefa 7 (top), 12 (bottom), 17 (bottom), 18 (bottom). All the illustrations were provided by John James.

INDEX